Who Built the Ark?

and other Questions

By Sally Ann Wright • Illustrated by Paola Bertolini Grudina

Who made the world?

God did!

Sea and sky, trees and plants,
fish and birds,
lions, tigers, and bears,
and people just like us:
so we could love him,
just as he loves us.

Who built the ark?

Noah!

He built a big boat
and filled it with animals
of every shape and color.
Then when the flood came,
God kept him and his family
and all the animals safe.

Who fought a giant?

David!

He wasn't a soldier.
He looked after his father's sheep.
He didn't have any armor,
and his weapon was a stone in a sling.
But he wasn't afraid.
David knew God would help him.

Who washed in a river?

Naaman!

He suffered from a horrible skin disease. His little servant girl told him to ask the prophet Elisha to help him.

Elisha told Naaman to wash seven times
in the River Jordan and he would be well.
He did – and God healed him!

Who was thrown to the lions?

Daniel!

He was taken away from his home
and made to live in a strange land
where he didn't have many friends.
But Daniel loved God and trusted him.
When his enemies threw him in the lions' den,
God closed the lions' mouths and saved him.

Who ran away?

Jonah!

He heard God call him,
but didn't want to do what he said!
He took a boat going the other way.
So God caused a storm
to stop him.
Jonah was swallowed by
a big fish.
But God kept him safe
until he was sorry for what
            he had done.

Who followed a star?

The wise men!

A new star meant a new king had been born.
So they traveled a long way
to bring him gifts.
He wasn't in the king's palace.
He wasn't wearing a crown.
But he was with his mother Mary.
The name of the new king was Jesus.

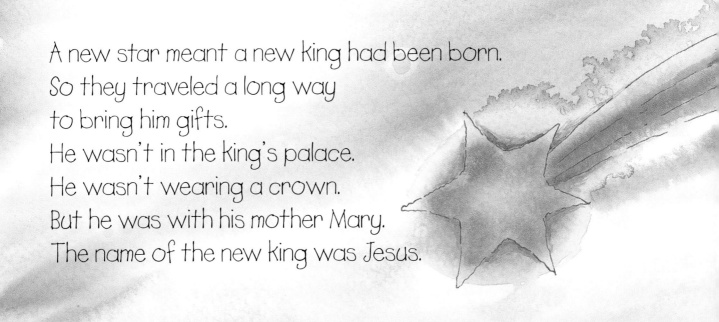

Who calmed a storm?

Jesus!

He went across Lake Galilee with his friends
in a little fishing boat after a very busy day.
Jesus was so tired, he fell asleep.
But a storm blew up that made the boat rock!
His friends were very frightened.
Then Jesus told the wind and the waves to be still,
and the lake was calm again.

Who threw away his stick?

Bartimaeus!

He sat by the roadside day after day,
begging for money because he couldn't see.
When Jesus came by, he called to him for help.
"How can I help you?" asked Jesus.

"I want to see again!" said Bartimaeus.
So Jesus healed him – and Bartimaeus threw away his stick
and was so happy, he followed Jesus.

Who climbed a tree?

Zacchaeus!

He was so small that he couldn't see Jesus
over the heads of the crowd.
So he climbed into the branches of a fig tree
until Jesus saw him and told him to come down.
Zacchaeus changed once he got to know Jesus.
He wanted to be kind to everyone around him.

Who saw the empty tomb?

Mary!

She had seen where Jesus' dead body had been laid,
and she went early in the morning to the garden,

bringing spices to anoint his body.
But she found the stone had been rolled away.
Jesus was alive and risen from the dead!

Who doubted Jesus was alive?

Thomas!

He was not with the other disciples
when they saw Jesus risen from the dead.
So Jesus came back to see him and talk to him.

He asked Thomas to touch his wounds.
Thomas knew then that this was Jesus.
He knelt and worshipped him.

Who jumped out of a boat?

Peter!

The disciples had been fishing all night
but had caught nothing.
Then they saw Jesus making breakfast on the shore.

He told them where to throw the net
and they caught 153 fish!
Peter splashed through the water to reach him
because he was so pleased to see Jesus again.

Stories can be found in the Bible as follows:
Who made the world? Genesis 1
Who built the ark? Genesis 6:11-22
Who fought a giant? 1 Samuel 17
Who washed in a river? 2 Kings 5:1-14
Who was thrown to the lions? Daniel 6:1-23
Who ran away? Jonah 1-2
Who followed a star? Matthew 2:1-11
Who calmed a storm? Luke 8:22-24
Who threw away his stick? Mark 10:46-52
Who climbed a tree? Luke 19:1-8
Who saw the empty tomb? John 20:1-18
Who doubted Jesus was alive? John 20:24-29
Who jumped out of a boat? John 21:1-14

Cataloging-in-Publication Data from the Library of Congress is available on request.

ISBN: 0-8091-6730-1

Published in the United States by Paulist Press
997 Macarthur Boulevard, Mahwah, NJ 07430

www.paulistpress.com

Printed and bound in Singapore